Introduction

1 Simple Treats 5

2 Special Treats 23

3 Chocolate Treats 41

Weights and measures 46

Index 48

contents

contents

introduction

Float blissfully on a cloud to seventh heaven with our divine desserts. Prepare to be enveloped in a celestial experience because our desserts look and taste truly angelic. The sweet tooth or the occasional indulger can bring these dreamy visions to life in their very own kitchen. A well-made dessert is a slice of heaven on earth.

Whether you seek an everyday treat or you want to spoil a good friend or family member, we have carefully selected this range for your ultimate enjoyment. Our sensational collection of recipes will draw the eye to feast on each unique shape and texture, from piping-hot apple pie that will be the toast of the county fair to chewy toffee that is enough to rival even Willy Wonka's famous fare. Our fabulous glossy pictures are a testament to just how much dessert making is the 'art of the masses' that can create a magnificent masterpiece from seemingly ordinary recipe ingredients. Simple things like flour, eggs, butter or sugar form the basis for delectable desserts of all descriptions that are blended and baked to perfection. They provide a window into another world

where all five senses are reeling. If food is meant to be enjoyed, then desserts would have to be the crown of the dinner table. Expect to smack a few eager hands hovering over the mixing bowl because we have some wonderful things in store for you!

So why the world's fascination with dessert? Perhaps it is the favourite part of any meal because after dining on a fabulous main you know the best is yet to grace your plate. After a savoury experience, a sweet sensation summons a new type of utopia for your tastebuds. Or perhaps, as one scientist has suggested, there exists a gene that makes an individual crave sweet substances at a deeper, biological level. So while the need for dessert may not have been created by culture, it has been the creativity found within each country that has produced delightful new discoveries to meet this shameless human need. With millions of dollars of desserts being consumed every year, it has become a staple of many a household.

Even with an increase in the choice of desserts on the restaurant menu, in the local bakery and in the supermarket freezer, there's just nothing like home cooking. Needless to say, sugar is one of baking's best assets. This affordable ingredient is the base for thousands of desserts from Sydney to San Francisco. It is found in many forms, from brown crystals used in sumptuous pudding sauces to the white powder used to dust tasty sponge cakes. But the results have one thing in common – they are distinctively sweet for that 'sugar rush' so many people seek. There is not a sensible restaurant

anywhere in the world that would not include a sugar-kissed dessert on their menu to consummate the dining experience. Like wine, dessert is meant to be enjoyed in moderation and the offerings range from simple to superior. There's always something new to try.

What makes homemade desserts distinct from their commercial counterparts is they are quite simply a delicacy beyond the call of duty. The homemade meal is an expectation of many families, but the dessert is an entirely different matter because it spoils where even the most carefully-crafted casserole cannot. Therein lies its advantage. No wonder it is the source of so many glowing compliments and the subject of so many requests. This recipe book offers a great opportunity to broaden your repertoire and bring a new sense of adventure into your cooking. Even the most dedicated homemaker can become bored with whipping up the family favourite, so now is the time to develop a new talent for dessert making. Try something different for dessert tonight or doggy-ear a page for a special occasion, such as a dinner party or a spouse's birthday. You put so much thought into a meal, so leave a lasting impression with a fantastic finale.

To streamline the baking process, we have rallied together a team of experts so you can have absolute confidence that your dessert with be just as delicious as you expect it to be when you first see its eye-bulging picture. Few people can throw together ingredients to create something mouth-watering so we've done all the hard work for you. All our recipes, whether old fashioned favourites or new taste trends, have been tested so that if you follow the instructions you will certainly have a licence to thrill. Out with the embarrassing flop, in with the enchanting ecstasy. Never before has making a dessert been so easy and so enjoyable. So bring the streets of gold right to your front door and bake up a storm in your kitchen today. Relish every morsel and bon apetit!

simple
treats

strawberry

Serves** 4* ***Preparation *25mins plus 15mins chilling and 15mins cooling*
Cooking *20mins* ***Calories*** *549* ***Fat*** *38g*

and cream treats

145g/5oz plain flour
20g/²⁄₃oz confectioners sugar, plus extra to dust
100g/3½oz unsalted butter, softened
finely grated rind of 1 small lemon, plus 1 tsp juice
145mL/5fl oz carton double or whipping cream
22g/8oz strawberries, halved
4 tbsp raspberry jam or redcurrant jelly to glaze

1 Preheat the oven to 190°C/375°F/Gas Mark 5. Sift the flour and sugar into a bowl. Rub in the butter and the lemon juice and knead lightly until the mixture forms a smooth dough. Cover with plastic wrap and refrigerate for 15 minutes.

2 Roll the dough out thinly on a lightly floured surface, divide into 4 and use to line 4 x 7½cm/3in loose-bottomed tartlet tins. Line with baking paper and baking beans and bake for 15 minutes. Remove the paper and beans and cook for another 3-5 minutes, until the pastry is golden. Leave to cool for 15 minutes, then remove from the tins.

3 Whip the cream with the lemon rind until it forms soft peaks. Spoon into the cases and top with the strawberries. Melt the jam or jelly over a gentle heat with 1 tablespoon of water, then press through a sieve and cool slightly. Spoon over the strawberries, then dust with icing sugar.

warm apricot brioches

4 individual brioches
6 fresh apricots, halved and stoned, or 12 canned apricot halves, drained
6 tbsp apricot conserve or jam
1 tbsp orange juice
4 small scoops vanilla ice cream

1 Preheat the oven. Slice the top off each brioche and set aside, then carefully hollow out the centres and discard. Place 3 apricot halves in the middle of each brioche.

2 Put the brioches and their tops onto a baking sheet and cook for 8 minutes or until heated through and slightly crispy. Meanwhile, gently heat the conserve or jam in a saucepan with the orange juice, stirring, until melted.

3 Place each brioche on a plate and top with a scoop of ice cream. Drizzle the conserve or jam mixture over, then replace the tops.

Note: For speed, looks and taste, these brioches are hard to beat. They're also versatile: try using crème fraîche instead of ice cream, and quartered peaches rather than apricots.

Serves 4 **Preparation** 30mins **Cooking** 8-10mins **Calories** 122 **Fat** 4g

grilled peaches with fromage frais

6 ripe peaches

55/2oz amaretti biscuits, roughly crushed

200g/7oz low-fat fromage frais

1 tbsp confectioners sugar

1 Cut each peach in half from top to bottom and, using both hands, twist to loosen the flesh from the stone. Carefully remove the stone with the point of a knife.

2 Place the peach halves, cut-side up, in a shallow heatproof dish. Divide the amaretti biscuits between the peach halves and top each with a large spoonful of fromage frais.

3 Preheat the grill to medium. Grill the peaches for 5 minutes or until the tops are lightly browned, then sprinkle with a little sugar. Increase the heat and grill for another 2 minutes or until the sugar browns slightly.

NOTE: Fromage fraise is strawberry cream cheese which should be available at your favourite delicatessen or supermarket.

Serves 4   **Preparation** 5mins   **Cooking** 7mins   **Calories** 164   **Fat** 6g

strawberry trifle

1 Divide the biscuits or sponge halves between 4 x 145mL/5oz ramekins and spoon over the Madeira, sherry or kirsch.

2 Whip the cream until it forms soft peaks, then fold in the custard and strawberries. Divide the cream mixture between the ramekins. Smooth the tops and sprinkle over a thick layer of sugar.

3 Meanwhile, preheat the grill to high. Place the ramekins under the grill for 2-3 minutes, until the sugar caramelises. Leave to cool, then refrigerate for 2 hours before serving.

Note: Strawberries and crushed almond biscuits in a light, creamy custard, covered by a layer of caramelised sugar – it's easy and tastes every bit as good as it sounds.

85g/3oz amaretti biscuits, roughly crushed, or 2 trifle sponges, cut in half
2 tbsp Madeira, sweet sherry or kirsch
85mL/3fl oz whipping or double cream
85mL/3fl oz ready-made custard
100g/3½oz strawberries, hulled and halved
3 tbsp demerara sugar

Serves 4   **Preparation** 15mins plus 2 hrs chilling   **Cooking** 3mins
Calories 1236   **Fat** 11g

bruleé

85mL/3fl oz whipping or double cream

145mL/5fl oz condensed milk

grated rind and juice of 2 limes

18cm/7in sweet pastry case

280g/9oz pack meringue mix

Serves 6
Preparation 25 mins plus 1 hr chilling
Cooking 4mins
Calories 241
Fat 12g

cheat's key lime pie

1 Whip the cream until it forms soft peaks. Gently fold in the condensed milk, lime rind and juice. Spoon the mixture into the pastry case and refrigerate for 1 hour – the mixture is quite loose at first but firms up when refrigerated.

2 Meanwhile, make the meringue topping according to the packet instructions, whisking until it forms stiff peaks (this is best done with an electric whisk).

3 Preheat the grill to medium. Spoon the meringue over the cream mixture. Grill for 2-4 minutes, until the meringue turns golden. Serve either warm or cold.

Note: This tangy alternative to lemon meringue pie comes from the Florida Keys. It's still on the menus of many of the seafront cafés. One bite, and you'll think you're there!

cranachan
with raspberries

30g/1oz butter

40g/1⅓oz soft dark brown sugar

115g/4oz porridge oats

200g/7oz fromage frais

145ml/5fl oz carton whipping cream

1-2 tbsp clear honey, plus extra for trickling (optional)

1-2 tbsp whisky

225g/8oz raspberries

2 tbsp confectioners sugar

1 Preheat the oven. Melt the butter and sugar in a small saucepan over low heat, then stir in the oats until well mixed. Turn onto a baking sheet and spread out. Bake for 15 minutes, stirring halfway through, until lightly toasted. Transfer to a plate and leave to cool while you prepare the cream mixture.

2 Beat the fromage frais until smooth. Whisk the cream until it forms soft peaks, then fold into the fromage frais with 1-2 tablespoons of honey and whisky to taste. Toss the fruit in the icing sugar.

3 Spoon the fromage frais mixture into bowls, top with the oats and finish with the raspberries. Trickle over the extra honey, if desired.

Serves 4   **Preparation** 15mins   **Cooking** 20mins   **Calories** 208   **Fat** 13g

mango oat crunch

2 mangoes
55g/2oz butter
30g/1oz golden sugar
125g/4oz porridge oats
200g/7oz carton full fat soft cheese
200g/7oz carton crème fraîche
juice of ½ lemon
4 tbsp clear honey

1 To prepare the mangoes, slice the two fatter 'cheeks' of the mangoes from either side of the stone. Cut a criss-cross pattern across the flesh of each piece to divide into small cubes, then push the skin upwards from the centre and carefully slice off the cubes into a bowl.

2 Melt the butter and sugar in a saucepan and add the porridge oats. Cook over medium heat for 4–5 minutes, stirring all the time, until the oats are just golden and toasted. Leave to cool slightly.

3 Mix together the soft cheese and crème fraîche in a bowl, add the lemon juice and 2 tablespoons of the honey and combine well. Spoon the oats into individual glasses or serving bowls. Add a layer of the cream mixture, top with the mango, then drizzle over the remaining honey and serve immediately. Alternatively, fold the mango and oats into the cream and serve all combined in glasses or bowls.

Serves 4   **Preparation** 10mins **Cooking** 5mins   **Calories** 616 **Fat** 31g

pear
and almond flan

- 2 large, firm pears, peeled, cored and sliced
- 1 tsp lemon juice
- 55g/2oz confectioners sugar
- 200g/7oz shortcrust pastry, defrosted if frozen
- 3-4 tbsp apricot or plum jelly
- 55g/2oz soft margarine
- 1 medium egg
- 55g/2oz all-purpose flour
- 55g/2oz ground almonds
- 30g/1oz flaked almonds
- confectioners sugar to dust

Serves 6
Preparation 25mins
Cooking 1hr
Calories 240
Fat 16g

1 Preheat the oven to 180°C/350°F/Gas Mark 4. Toss the pears with the lemon juice and 1 teaspoon of the confectioners sugar.

2 Roll the pastry out thinly on a lightly floured surface and line a 20cm/8in loose-bottomed flan tin. Refrigerate for 10 minutes. Line the pastry with baking paper and a layer of baking beans and cook for 15 minutes. Remove the paper and beans and cook for another 5 minutes or until lightly golden. Leave to cool for 5 minutes.

3 Spread the jelly over the pastry and top with the pears. Beat the margarine and remaining sugar until pale and creamy, then add the egg, flour and ground almonds and beat to a soft, dropping consistency. Spoon the mixture over the pears, sprinkle with flaked almonds and cook for 30 minutes or until set and golden. Cool for 10 minutes, then transfer to a plate and dust with icing sugar.

apple roll-ups

1 To make the batter, blend the flour, milk, egg, orange rind and melted butter until smooth in a food processor or using a hand blender. Leave it to rest for 20 minutes.

2 Meanwhile, make the filling. Place the apples, cinnamon and 1 tablespoon of water into a small saucepan, cover, and cook gently for 5-7 minutes, stirring occasionally, until the apples have softened.

3 Melt just enough butter to cover the base of a 18cm/7in non-stick frying pan. Pour in a quarter of the batter and tilt the pan so that it covers the base. Cook for 1-2 minutes on each side, until golden. Keep warm and repeat to make 3 more pancakes, greasing the pan when necessary.

4 Place 2 pancakes on each plate. Fill with the apple mixture and carefully roll up. Serve with maple syrup.

Note: Roll up, roll up... for these hot apple-filled pancakes, served with maple syrup. Try them with a generous dollop of creamy yoghurt or a scoop of vanilla ice cream.

55g/2oz plain flour

145mL/5fl oz full-fat milk

1 medium egg

finely grated rind of $\frac{1}{2}$ small orange

30g/1oz butter, melted, plus extra for frying

maple syrup to serve

For the filling

2 eating apples, peeled, cored and chopped

$\frac{1}{2}$ tsp ground cinnamon

Serves 2　***Preparation*** 15mins plus 20mins resting
Cooking 25mins　***Calories*** 348　***Fat*** 18g

100g/3½oz butterscotch sweets

485g/16fl oz tub vanilla ice cream

312g/11oz can mandarins, drained

3 chocolate flakes

hop scotch

1 Place the butterscotch sweets into a strong plastic bag. Roughly crush with a rolling pin.

2 Place the ice cream in a large bowl and mash with a fork. Mix in the crushed butterscotch. Return to the container and freeze for 1-2 hours.

3 Transfer the ice cream to the fridge for 20 minutes before serving to soften slightly. Place the mandarins in sundae glasses, together with 2 scoops of ice cream. Crush one of the chocolate flakes and sprinkle over the top of the ice cream. Cut the remaining flakes in half and push 1 into each serving.

Serves 4 **Preparation** 10mins plus 2hrs freezing and 20mins cooling
Calories 533 **Fat** 27g

banana drama

30g/1oz butter

1 apple, peeled, cored and sliced

2 bananas, thickly sliced

finely grated rind of 1/4 lemon and 1/2 tsp lemon juice

30g/1oz soft light brown sugar

1/4 tsp ground cinnamon

1 Melt the butter in a medium-sized saucepan. Add the apple and cook over medium heat for 3 minutes, turning once, until softened. Add the bananas, stir gently, and cook for a further 2 minutes or until golden.

2 Add the lemon rind and juice, sugar and cinnamon to the pan. Cook for 2-3 minutes, stirring gently, until the sauce turns golden and coats the fruit.

Note; Hot, gooey caramel sauce poured over chunks of banana and slices of sticky apple – it's guaranteed to get children eating fruit. Serve it with some vanilla ice cream.

Serves 2 ***Preparation*** 5mins ***Cooking*** 8mins ***Calories*** 244 ***Fat*** 10g

pear, raspberry

Serves 6 **Preparation** 15mins **Calories** 276 **Fat** 15g

and almond sponge

200mL/7fl oz dry or slightly sweet white wine

2-3 strips lemon rind, pared with a vegetable peeler, and juice of one lemon

2 tbsp clear honey or sugar

4 whole cloves

4 large ripe pears, peeled, quartered and cored

100g/3½oz butter, softened

55g/2oz powder sugar

grated rind of ½ orange

3 eggs, lightly beaten

145g/5oz ground almonds

2 tsp orange-flower water or natural vanilla extract (optional)

115g/4oz punnet fresh raspberries

sifted confectioners sugar to dust

1 Preheat the oven to 180°C/350°F/ Gas Mark 4. Place the wine, lemon rind and juice, honey or sugar and cloves in a saucepan. Bring to the boil, then simmer, uncovered, for 5 minutes or until reduced slightly. Add the pears, cover and cook for 5 minutes or until tender.

Transfer the pears to a dish, drain and cool. Strain the cooking liquid, discarding the lemon rind and cloves, and reserve.

2 Beat the butter, sugar and orange rind until light and fluffy (this is easiest with an electric whisk). Gradually add the eggs, ground almonds, orange-flower water or vanilla, if using, and beat until smooth.

3 Arrange the pears in a 25cm/10in flan dish. Sprinkle over half the raspberries and top with the egg mixture, smoothing with the back of a spoon. Bake for 25-30 minutes, until firm to the touch.

4 Meanwhile, place the reserved liquid into a small saucepan and bring to the boil. Boil for 5 minutes or until reduced to about 3 tablespoons. Increase the oven temperature to 230°C/450°F/ Gas Mark 8. Spoon the liquid over the flan and bake for 5 minutes longer or until golden. Cool slightly, then decorate with the remaining raspberries and dust with confectioners sugar.

baked
passionfruit custards

| 4 large eggs, beaten |
| 4 tbsp confectioners sugar |
| 145mL/5fl oz coconut milk |
| pinch of salt |
| 2 passionfruit |

1 Preheat the oven to 180°C/350°F/Gas Mark 4. Whisk together the eggs, sugar, coconut milk and salt until smooth, then pour into 4 ramekins.

2 Halve 1 passionfruit, scoop out the pulp and seeds and divide between the 4 custard-filled ramekins. Place them in a deep baking dish.

3 Pour boiling water into the baking dish to come three-quarters of the way up the sides of the ramekins. Bake the custards for 40 minutes. Serve warm or cold with the pulp and seeds from the remaining passionfruit spooned over the top.

Note: This creamy dessert is totally delicious. The passio fruit gives the custard a distinctive sweetness and the seeds add texture, but you can use fresh mango if you prefer.

Serves 4 **Preparation** 10mins **Cooking** 40mins **Calories** 226 **Fat** 14g

2 special treats

date and walnut

1 Preheat the oven to 180°C/350°F/ Gas Mark 4. Simmer the dates and orange juice in a saucepan for 4-5 minutes, until the liquid is just absorbed. Stir in the rind, walnuts and cinnamon. Brush a shallow 20cm/ 8in square tin with butter. Keeping the remaining pastry covered, lay 1 sheet in the tin and brush with butter. Top with another sheet and brush again. Repeat to form 8 layers in total.

2 Spread half the date mixture over the pastry and top with 2 buttered sheets. Spread with the remaining filling and finish with 2 more buttered sheets. Tuck in the edges, score a diamond pattern on top and sprinkle with sesame seeds. Bake for 30 minutes or until golden, then reduce the oven to 150°C/300°F/ Gas Mark 2 and bake for 30-40 minutes.

3 Simmer the honey, lemon juice and 200mL/7fl oz of water in a pan for 10-15 minutes, until reduced by half, then leave to cool for 20 minutes. Pour over the baklava and cool for 1 hour before slicing.

225g/8oz dried stoned dates, chopped
finely grated rind and juice of 1 orange
115g/4oz walnut pieces, chopped
½ tsp ground cinnamon
75g/2½oz butter, melted
12 sheets fresh filo pastry, trimmed to fit the tin
1 tsp sesame seeds
145g/5oz clear honey
juice of ½ lemon

***Serves** 6 **Preparation** 30mins*
***Cooking** 1½ hours **Calories** 514 **Fat** 30g*

baklava

date puddings with

sticky toffee sauce

85g (3oz) butter, softened, plus extra for greasing

100g/3½oz stoned dates chopped

100g/3½oz soft light brown sugar

½ tsp vanilla essence

2 large eggs

100g/3½oz plain wholemeal flour

1½ tsp baking powder

1 very ripe banana, mashed

For the toffee sauce

85g/3oz soft dark brown sugar

55g/2oz butter

2 tbsp single cream

1 Preheat the oven to 180°C/350°F/Gas Mark 4. Grease 4 x 200mL (7fl oz) pudding basins or ramekins with butter. Cover the dates with boiling water and soak for 10 minutes to soften.

2 Beat the butter, sugar and vanilla essence until pale and creamy. Beat in the eggs, then fold in the flour and baking powder. Strain the dates and blend to a purée in a food processor, or mash with a fork. Stir into the mixture with the banana.

3 Spoon the mixture into the basins or ramekins, almost to their tops, and place on a baking sheet. Bake for 20 minutes or until well risen and just firm to the touch. Cool for 5 minutes, then loosen the puddings with a knife and invert onto plates.

4 To make the sauce, place the sugar, butter and cream in a pan and heat gently for 5 minutes or until syrupy. Pour over the puddings to serve.

Note: Sponge pudding, bananas, dates, and a sticky toffee sauce...what a great combination! You can serve it on its own or with a big scoop of good vanilla ice cream.

Serves 4
Preparation 20mins plus 10mins soaking and 5mins cooling
Cooking 25mins
Calories 633
Fat 32g

hedgegrow pie

1 Preheat the oven to 200°C/400°F/Gas Mark 6. Place the fruit and sugar into a saucepan. Simmer, covered, for 1-2 minutes, until the fruit begins to soften, then set aside for 5 minutes to cool. Strain the fruit, reserving the juice.

2 Set aside a small piece of pastry to make the decorations. Roll out the remaining pastry on a floured surface into a rough circle, about 18cm/7in across. Place on a non-stick baking sheet. Place the fruit in the centre of the pastry and gather up the edges, leaving the top slightly open. Brush the top of the pastry with a little of the egg.

3 Roll out the reserved pastry and cut out acorn, leaf and blackberry shapes. Brush the shapes with egg and stick them onto the sides of the pie. Bake for 25 minutes or until the pastry is golden. Remove from the oven. Lightly dust with confectioners sugar. Serve with the reserved fruit juice, if liked.

Note: This fruit pie is delicious and great fun to make. Children will love it even more if you let them go berry picking and help you make the pastry decorations.

255g/9oz fresh or frozen mixed fruits, such as blackberries, raspberries, blueberries and strawberries

30g/1oz confectioners sugar, plus extra for dusting

145g/5oz shortcrust pastry

1 egg, beaten, for glazing

Serves 2   **Preparation** 25 mins plus 5mins cooling
Cooking 30mins   **Calories** 437   **Fat** 26g

luxury tiramisu

12 sponge fingers
145mL/5fl oz strong black coffee
145mL/5fl oz coffee liqueur, such as Tia Maria
285mL/10oz carton double cream
145mL/5fl oz mascarpone
55g/2oz confectioners sugar
55g/2oz plain chocolate, grated, plus extra shavings to decorate

1 Line the base and sides of a 450g/16oz loaf tin with cling film. Lay 4 sponge fingers in the tin. Mix together the coffee and liqueur and pour one-third of the mixture into the tin. Put the rest of the sponge fingers into a shallow bowl and pour over the remaining coffee mixture.

2 Whip half of the cream until it forms soft peaks. Fold in the mascarpone and sugar. Spread half of the mixture over the sponge fingers in the tin. Sprinkle with 30g/1oz of grated chocolate.

3 Top with a layer of the soaked sponge fingers, then add the rest of the cream mixture and grated chocolate. Finish with another layer of soaked sponge fingers and refrigerate for 2 hours. Invert the tiramisu onto a plate and remove the cling film. Whip the rest of the cream and spread over the top and sides. Decorate with the chocolate shavings.

Serves 6 **Preparation** 20mins plus 5mins soaking and 2hrs chilling
Calories 519 **Fat** 37g

upside down apple tart

- 100g/3½oz plain flour
- 1 tbsp cornstarch
- pinch of salt
- 1 tbsp confectioners sugar
- 145g/5oz unsalted butter, softened
- 55g/2oz soft light brown sugar
- pinch of ground cinnamon
- 2 cooking apples, or 4 eating apples, peeled, cored and sliced

1 Preheat the oven to 180°C/350°F/Gas Mark 4. Sift the flour with the cornflour, salt and confectioners sugar, then mix in 100g/3½oz of the butter until the mixture forms a soft ball. Shape into a round, cover with plastic wrap and refrigerate for 10 minutes.

2 Place the brown sugar, the remaining butter and the cinnamon in an ovenproof frying pan or 20cm/8in shallow non-stick cake tin. Heat in a saucepan over heat for 3 minutes or until the sugar turns syrupy.

3 Arrange the apples in the tin. Roll out the pastry between 2 sheets of baking paper until it is just larger than the pan or tin. Place the pastry on top of the apples, tucking the edge into the inside of the pan or tin. Bake for 35-40 minutes, until the pastry is crisp and golden. Cool for 10 minutes, then invert onto a serving plate.

Serves 6 **Preparation** 25mins plus 10mins chilling and 10mins cooling **Cooking** 40mins **Calories** 317 **Fat** 21g

hazelnut
pancakes with strawberries

4 medium eggs
125mL/4½ofl oz half-fat milk
3 tbsp clear honey or sugar
100g/3½oz roasted chopped hazelnuts
100g/3½oz plain flour
1 tsp baking powder
1 tsp ground cinnamon
pinch of salt
3 tbsp melted butter

To serve

170mL/6floz maple syrup
115g/4oz tub clotted cream
strawberries fo garnish

1 Beat the eggs with the milk and honey or sugar until light and fluffy. Gradually add the hazelnuts, flour, baking powder, cinnamon andsalt, then beat to a smooth batter.

2 Heat a small, heavy-based frying pan, then brush with ½ teaspoon of the melted butter. Drop in 2 tablespoons of the batter, then quickly tilt the pan to cover the base. Fry for 1-2 minutes, until golden, turn over and fry for a further minute or until browned. Repeat until all the batter has been used (about 18 pancakes), greasing the pan as necessary.

3 Serve the pancakes drizzled with maple syrup and served with clotted cream and strawberries.

Serves 4   **Preparation** 10mins   **Cooking** 2-30mins   **Calories** 760 **Fat** 60g

brazil nut
shortbreads with strawberries

For the shortbread

30g/1oz brazil nuts

55g/2oz golden sugar

115g/4oz plain white flour

75g/2½ oz butter, softened

2 medium egg yolks

For the filling

1 tsp grated orange rind, plus extra, to decorate

225g/8oz carton extra thick cream

225g/8oz punnet strawberries, hulled and sliced

4 tbsp strawberry jam

Serves 4 **Preparation** 15mins **Cooking** 10-15mins **Calories** 560 **Fat** 45g

1 Place the nuts and sugar in a food processor and whizz until fine, add the flour and butter and whizz until it resembles fine breadcrumbs. Add the egg yolks and pulse until the mixture forms a soft dough. (taking care not to over-process.) Bring the mixture together to form a ball, then cover with plastic wrap and chill for 20 minutes.

2 Preheat the oven. On a lightly floured surface, roll out the dough to 5mm/½in thick and stamp out eight 7½cm/3in rounds with a biscuit cutter, re-rolling as necessary. Place on a greased baking tray and bake for 10–12 minutes, until lightly golden. Cool on a wire rack.

3 Fold the orange rind into the cream. Place a small amount of cream on a biscuit, top with strawberries, another biscuit, then more cream and strawberries. Warm the jam in a small saucepan, then drizzle it over the top. Decorate with orange rind. Repeat with the remaining biscuits.

lemon
& ginger syllabus

1 Whip the cream until slightly thickened. Gradually whisk in the ginger wine or white wine, lemon rind and juice and the sugar.

2 Slice one piece of stem ginger into matchsticks and set aside. Finely chop the remaining piece, then fold into the cream mixture.

3 Spoon the mixture into small glasses or bowls and refrigerate for 30 minutes. Decorate with the reserved stem ginger matchsticks and the mint.

Note: Serve this rich lemony pudding with crispy biscuits, such as langues de chats. Don't prepare the syllabus too far in advance, as it may start to separate after a few hours.

Serves 4
Preparation 1 mins
plus 30mins chilling
Calories 396
Fat 34g

285mL/10oz carton double cream

100mL/3½fl oz ginger wine or medium sweet white wine

finely grated rind and juice of 1 large lemon

55g/2oz confectioners sugar

2 pieces stem ginger in syrup, drained

fresh mint to decorate

summer pudding

with redcurrant sauce

1 Place the fruit, sugar and 3 tablespoons of water in a saucepan and simmer for 5 minutes or until the fruit has softened. Leave to cool slightly.

2 Line the base and sides of a 900mL/35fl oz pudding basin with 6 slices of the bread, cutting to fit and making sure there are no gaps. Strain the fruit, reserving the juice, then add the fruit to the basin. Cover with the remaining bread to form a lid. Spoon over 3-4 tablespoons of the reserved juice.

3 Place a plate on top of the bread, with a weight, such as a large can, on it. Place in the fridge for 2-3 hours to let the juices soak through the bread.

4 For the sauce, strain the reserved juice into a pan, then add the redcurrant jelly. Simmer for 2-3 minutes, stirring, until the jelly has melted. Invert the pudding onto a plate and serve with the redcurrant sauce.

1kg/35g fresh or frozen mixed berry fruits
3 tbsp confectioners sugar
8 slices white or wholemeal bread, crusts removed
2 tbsp redcurrant jelly

Serves 6   **Preparation** 20mins plus 3hrs chilling
Cooking 8mins   **Calories** 177   **Fat** trace

caramelised
rice pudding with apricots

- 75g/2½oz pudding rice
- 200g/7oz confectioners sugar
- 2 vanilla pods, 1 split in half lengthways
- 30g/1oz unsalted butter
- 600mL/21fl oz full-fat milk
- 145mL/5oz carton double cream
- 2 strips lemon rind and juice of 1 lemon
- 255g/9oz ready-to-eat dried apricots
- 1-2 tbsp orange liqueur, such as Cointreau

1 Place the rice into a saucepan, cover with water and boil for 5 minutes. Drain. Return the rice to the pan with 45g/1½oz of the sugar, the split vanilla pod, butter and milk. Simmer for 45-60 minutes, stirring often, until thickened. Transfer to a bowl and cool for 20 minutes. Remove the vanilla pod and scrape the seeds into the rice. Discard the pod. Whisk the cream until it forms soft peaks, then fold into the rice.

2 Meanwhile, place 100g/3½oz of the sugar into a saucepan with the lemon strips, remaining vanilla pod and 200mL/7floz of water. Heat, stirring, for 3 minutes or until the sugar dissolves. Add the apricots and cook for 20 minutes to reduce the syrup.

3 Place the apricots into 4 ramekins, add the lemon juice, liqueur and syrup, then cool for 5 minutes. Top with the rice pudding, then refrigerate for 1 hour. Preheat the grill to high. Sprinkle the puddings with the rest of the sugar. Grill for 1-2 minutes, until the sugar caramelises, then cool for a few minutes.

Serves 4   ***Preparation*** 30mins ***Cooking*** 2hrs ***Calories*** 660 ***Fat*** 60g

1 large egg
100g/3½oz plain flour, sifted
pinch of salt
245mL/8floz half-fat milk
30g/1oz butter, melted
sunflower oil for greasing
2 large, firm bananas, sliced
3 tbsp Madeira, dessert wine or 2 tablespoon Drambuie
2-3 tsp demerara sugar

caramelised
rice pudding with apricots

1 Beat the egg, flour, salt and a little milk to a smooth paste. Gradually mix in the remaining milk, then stir in the melted butter.

2 Brush a non-stick, medium-sized frying pan with the oil and heat until very hot. Pour in 2-3 tablespoons of batter, swirling to cover the base of the pan. Cook the pancakes for 1-2 minutes on each side, until golden. Repeat to make 7 more, keeping the pancakes warm and layering them between sheets of baking paper to stop them sticking.

3 Preheat the grill to high. Wipe the pan, add the bananas and Madeira, wine or Drambuie and heat through gently, stirring.

4 When most of the liquid has evaporated, place a spoonful of the banana mixture on each pancake, fold it into quarters and place in a flameproof dish. Sprinkle with the sugar and grill until the tops of the pancakes are golden and lightly caramelised.

Serves 4 **Preparation** 10mins **Cooking** 20mins **Calories** 324 **Fat** 16g

3
chocolate
treats

little pots

# of chocolate

2x100g/3½oz bars luxury continental plain chocolate, broken into squares

145mL/5fl oz milk

2 tbsp brandy

1 egg

2 egg yolks

1 tsp natural vanilla extract

255mL/9fl oz carton double cream

2 tbsp caster sugar

4 tbsp Greek yoghurt

grated nutmeg to decorate

1 Preheat the oven. Place the chocolate, milk and brandy in a small saucepan. Cook over a low heat, stirring occasionally, for 5-6 minutes, until just melted, do not allow it to boil. Remove from the heat.

2 In a bowl, beat the egg, egg yolks, vanilla extract, cream and sugar until evenly combined. Quickly add to the chocolate mixture, mixing until smooth.

3 Divide the mixture evenly between 4x200mL/7fl oz ramekins. Place on a double layer of newspaper in a baking pan and pour in just enough boiling water to reach halfway up the sides of the dishes. Bake for 35-40 minutes or until lightly set. Remove and leave to cool for 30 minutes, then place in the fridge for 1 hour. Top with the yoghurt and grated nutmeg to serve.

Serves 4 **Preparation** 20mins **Cooking** 45mins **Calories** 563 **Fat** 38g

sticky chocolate and

1 Preheat the oven. Grease the base and sides of an 18cm/7in loose-bottomed cake tin and line with baking paper. Melt the chocolate and butter in a bowl set over a saucepan of simmering water, stirring. Cool slightly.

2 Meanwhile, press 75g/2½oz raspberries through a sieve. Whisk the egg yolks and sugar until pale and creamy, then mix in the almonds, cocoa, flour, melted chocolate and sieved raspberries.

3 Whisk the egg whites until they form stiff peaks (this is best done with an electric whisk). Fold a little into the chocolate mixture to loosen, then fold in the remainder. Spoon into the tin and cook for 25 minutes or until risen and just firm. Cool for 1 hour.

4 For the sauce, sieve the raspberries, then stir in the sugar, if using. Remove the cake from the tin and dust with the confectioners sugar. Serve with the sauce, decorated with mint and raspberries.

75g/2½oz unsalted butter, plus extra for greasing

75g/2½oz plain chocolate, broken into chunks

75g/2½oz fresh or frozen raspberries, defrosted if frozen, plus extra to decorate

2 medium eggs, separated

55g/2oz confectioners sugar

30g/1oz ground almonds

30g/1oz cocoa powder, sifted

30g/1oz plain flour, sifted

confectioners sugar to dust and fresh mint to decorate

For the sauce

145g/5oz fresh or frozen raspberries, defrosted if frozen

1 tbsp confectioners sugar (optional)

raspberry slice

Serves 6   **Preparation** 30mins   **Cooking** 25mins   **Calories** 319   **Fat** 24g

weights and measures

quick converter

Metric	Imperial
5mm	1/4 in
1cm	1/2 in
2cm	3/4 in
2 1/2 cm	1 in
5cm	2 in
10 1/2 cm	4 in
15cm	6 in
20cm	8 in
23cm	9 in
25cm	10 in
30cm	12 in

metric cups and spoons

Metric	Cups	Imperial
60mL	1/4 cup	2 fl oz
80mL	1/3 cup	2 1/2 fl oz
125mL	1/2 cup	4 fl oz
250mL	1 cup	8 fl oz
Metric	**Spoons**	
1 1/4 mL	1/4 teaspoon	
2 1/2 mL	1/2 teaspoon	
5mL	1 teaspoon	
20mL	1 tablespoon	

measuring liquids

Metric	Imperial	Cups
30mL	1 fl oz	
55mL	2 fl oz	1/4 cup
85mL	3 fl oz	
115mL	4 fl oz	1/2 cup
150mL	5 1/4 fl oz	
170mL	6 fl oz	2/3 cup
185mL	6 1/2 fl oz	
200mL	7 fl oz	
225mL	8 fl oz	1 cup
285mL	10 fl oz	
370mL	13 fl oz	
400mL	14 fl oz	
455mL	16 fl oz	2 cups
570mL	20 fl oz	
1 litre	35.3 fl oz	4 cups

oven temperatures

°C	°F	Gas Mark
120	250	1/4
140	275	1
150	300	2
160	326	3
180	350	4
190	375	5
200	400	6
220	425	7
240	475	8
250	500	9

measuring dry ingredients

Metric	Imperial
15g	$^1/_2$oz
20g	$^2/_3$oz
30g	1oz
55g	2oz
85g	3oz
115g	4oz
125g	4$^1/_2$oz
140g	5oz
170g	6oz
200g	7oz
225g	8oz ($^1/_2$lb)
255g	9oz
315g	11oz
370g	13oz
400g	14oz
425g	15oz
455g	16oz (1lb)
680g	1 lb 8oz
1kg	2.2lb
1$^1/_2$ kg	3.3lb

index

Apple dumplings with butter scotch	26
Apple roll-ups	17
Baked passionfruit custards	22
Banana drama	19
Brazil nut shortbreads with strawberries	33
Caramelised banana pancakes	40
Cheat's Key Lime Pie	12
Chocolate Treats	41
Cranachan with raspberries	13
Date and Walnut Baklava	24
Grilled peaches with fromage frais	9
Hazelnut pancakes with strawberries	32
Hedgegrow Pie	28
Hop Scotch	18
Lemon & ginger syllabus	34
Little pots of chocolate	42
Luxury tiramisu	30
Mango oat crunch	14
Pear and Almond flan	15
Pear, raspberry and almond sponge	20
Simple Treats	5
Special Treats	23
Sticky chocolate and raspberry slice	45
Strawberry and cream tarlets	6
Strawberry trifle brulee	10
Warm apricot brioches	8
Three berry fruit salad in pastry twists	36
Upside down apple tart	31
Weights and measures	31